Joe Mauer

ABDO
Publishing Company

Big
Buddy BOOKS
Buddy Bios

by **Sarah Tieck**

VISIT US AT

www.abdopublishing.com

Published by ABDO Publishing Company, 8000 West 78th Street, Edina, Minnesota 55439.

Printed in the United States of America, North Mankato, Minnesota.
102010
012011

 PRINTED ON RECYCLED PAPER

Coordinating Series Editor: Rochelle Baltzer
Contributing Editors: Megan M. Gunderson, BreAnn Rumsch, Marcia Zappa
Graphic Design: Maria Hosley
Cover Photograph: *Getty Images*: Jed Jacobsohn.
Interior Photographs/Illustrations: *AP Photo*: Mark Avery (p. 23), Paul Battaglia (p. 9), File (p. 23), Nati Harnik
        (p. 27), Jae C. Hong (p. 19), Andy King (p. 21), Charles Krupa, File (p. 23), Jim Mone (pp. 9, 13), Paul Sancya
        (p. 17), Jennifer Simonson/Star Tribune (pp. 5, 7), Eric Stromgren/Bemidji Pioneer (p. 29), John Suart (p. 20);
        Getty Images: Michael Buckner (p. 25); Ezra Shaw (p. 14); *Icon SMI*: Vince Muzik (p. 11).

Library of Congress Cataloging-in-Publication Data

Tieck, Sarah, 1976-
  Joe Mauer : baseball superstar / Sarah Tieck.
    p. cm. -- (Big buddy biographies)
  ISBN 978-1-61714-705-0
  1. Mauer, Joe, 1983---Juvenile literature. 2. Baseball players--United States--Biography--Juvenile literature. I. Title.
  GV865.M376T54 2011
  796.357092--dc22
  [B]
                            2010032596

Joe Mauer

Contents

Did you know...

A catcher is an important part of a team's defense. Catchers crouch, or bend low, behind home plate. They catch pitches and help get players out. Catchers also call pitches.

From a young age, Joe showed great talent as a baseball player.

Baseball Star

Joe Mauer is a famous **athlete**. He is a Major League Baseball (MLB) player. Joe is a talented, popular catcher for the Minnesota Twins. He is known for his swing.

Family Ties

Joseph Patrick Mauer was born on April 19, 1983, in St. Paul, Minnesota. His parents are Jake and Teresa Mauer. Joe has two older brothers named Jake and Billy.

The Mauers are a close family.
They often attend events together.

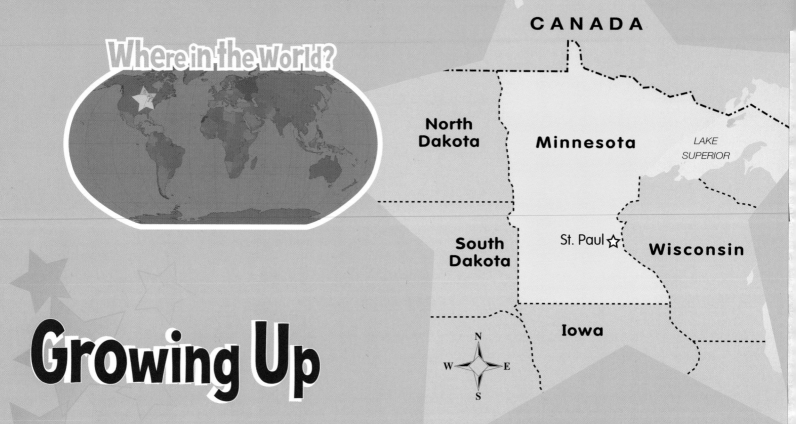

CANADA

North
Dakota

Minnesota

LAKE
SUPERIOR

South
Dakota

St. Paul ☆

Wisconsin

Iowa

N
W — E
S

Growing Up

Joe grew up in St. Paul. He spent time with friends and family. They loved to watch and play many different sports. They especially liked watching the Minnesota Twins play baseball.

Joe and his brothers often played baseball. To keep playing in winter, they even practiced in their basement! Their dad made a special machine to practice hitting.

Joe sees his family often. They enjoy attending games.

Did you know...

After Joe became a popular baseball player, people wanted to buy his dad's hitting machine. It is now for sale.

Joe attended high school at Cretin-Derham Hall in St. Paul. He was a good student.

Joe played baseball for Cretin-Derham Hall. He was the team's catcher. As a batter, he struck out just once in three seasons!

Basketball and football also came naturally for Joe. He won several national sports awards. In 2001, he was the Gatorade National Player of the Year for football!

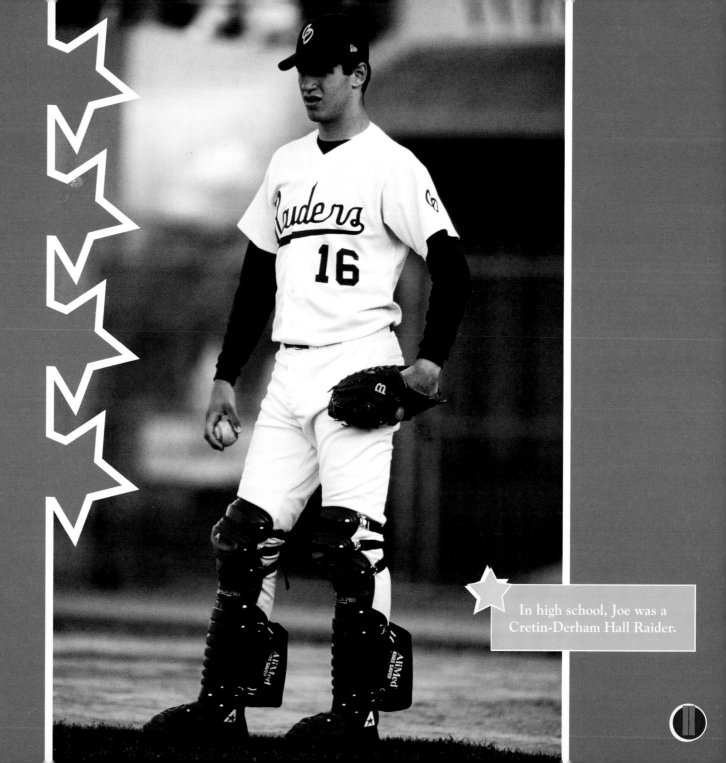

In high school, Joe was a
Cretin-Derham Hall Raider.

Going Pro

Joe considered playing football for Florida State University after high school. But then, he entered the 2001 MLB **draft**.

During the draft, the Minnesota Twins picked Joe. He was the first pick in the first round! So, Joe decided to play **professional** baseball instead of college football.

Did you know...

Joe was the first Minnesotan to be first pick at an MLB draft.

Many baseball fans were surprised when Joe was the number one draft choice. They expected a well-known college pitcher to be drafted first.

The Twins drafted both Joe and his brother Jake (*left*) in 2001. For a short time, they played on the same minor league team in Elizabethton, Tennessee.

Did you know...

The Minnesota Twins work with several minor league teams. Joe started out playing for the Elizabethton Twins.

Professional baseball players often start in the **minor leagues**. Joe began playing in the minor leagues in 2001.

There, Joe practiced and improved his game. After a few seasons, he was good enough to play in the major leagues.

Major Move

 Joe's first season as a Minnesota Twins player was 2004. Fans were very excited because Joe was from Minnesota. But, he played in less than half of the games because he hurt his knee.

 Joe gave his body time to heal. Then, he worked to strengthen his skills even more. He wanted to come back strong the next season.

Good At-Bat

In 2005, Joe returned to the team. He was ready to play! The Twins won the Central Division in 2006 and 2009. They came close in 2008. Winning meant they had the best record in their division and would go to the **play-offs**.

Joe became known for his style of hitting the ball. His swing is simple compared to other hitters. Some people call this a "pure" swing.

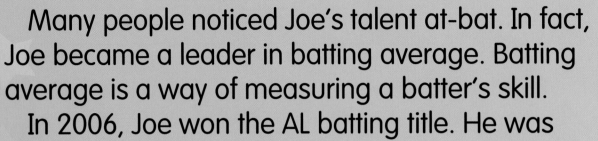

Many people noticed Joe's talent at-bat. In fact, Joe became a leader in batting average. Batting average is a way of measuring a batter's skill.

In 2006, Joe won the AL batting title. He was the first AL catcher to do this! In 2008 and 2009, Joe won two more batting titles.

The last Twins player to win the batting title was Kirby Puckett in 1989.

Former Twins players Tony Oliva (*left*) and Rod Carew (*right*) awarded Joe his first batting title trophy.

Team Players

Joe is good friends with his teammate Justin Morneau. Justin is a first baseman for the Twins. He and Joe spend time together on and off the field.

Some people believe Joe and Justin help each other play better. When the team is up to bat, they usually bat third and fourth. Then, they work together to score runs.

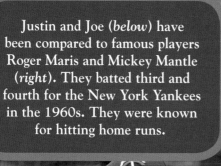

Justin and Joe (*below*) have been compared to famous players Roger Maris and Mickey Mantle (*right*). They batted third and fourth for the New York Yankees in the 1960s. They were known for hitting home runs.

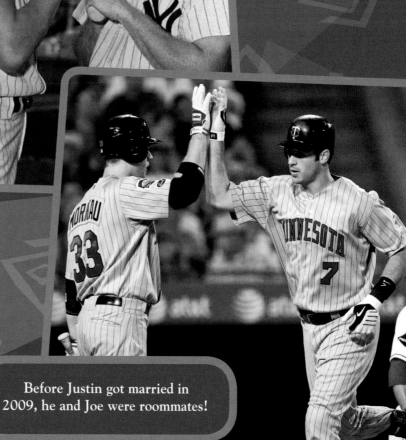

Before Justin got married in 2009, he and Joe were roommates!

Award Winner

Joe has received many honors for his skills. He has two Gold Glove and three Silver Slugger awards. Joe has played in the All-Star Game four times. That was just in his first six years as an MLB player!

Joe has become known throughout MLB as one of the best players. In 2009, he earned a special honor. Joe was named Most Valuable Player of the AL!

In an All-Star Game, the best AL players from different teams form one team. The AL team plays against a team of the best NL players.

Off the Field

Because of his talent, Joe has become popular. He attends events and meets fans. Reporters often **interview** Joe. And, stories about him appear in magazines and newspapers.

Joe is known for being quiet and calm. He is friendly, but **modest**. Joe works with groups to give back to his community. And, he enjoys spending time with family and friends at a cabin in Minnesota.

In his free time, Joe likes to play other sports such as golf.

Did you know...

Joe is a good dancer. When he was growing up, he learned to dance like Michael Jackson!

27

Buzz

The 2010 season was an exciting one for Joe. He signed with the Twins for another eight years! That year the Twins got a new ballpark. They also went to the AL **play-offs**. But, they lost to the New York Yankees.

Joe hopes to win the World Series someday. Many believe he has a bright **future**. Fans look forward to seeing what's next for Joe Mauer.

Joe is considered one of today's best MLB players!

Snapshot

⭐**Name**: Joseph Patrick Mauer

⭐**Birthday**: April 19, 1983

⭐**Birthplace**: St. Paul, Minnesota

⭐**Turned professional**: 2001

⭐**Plays with**: Minnesota Twins

⭐**Position**: Catcher

⭐**Number**: 7

Important Words

athlete a person who is trained or skilled in sports.

draft an event during which sports teams choose new players.

future (FYOO-chuhr) a time that has not yet occurred.

interview to ask someone a series of questions.

minor league (MEYE-nuhr LEEG) any group of professional baseball teams that compete at levels below that of major league teams.

modest not likely to brag about oneself.

play-off a set of games leading to a final match to find a winner.

professional (pruh-FEHSH-nuhl) working for money rather than for pleasure.

valuable of great use or service.

Web Sites

To learn more about Joe Mauer, visit ABDO Publishing Company online. Web sites about Joe Mauer are featured on our Book Links page. These links are routinely monitored and updated to provide the most current information available.

www.abdopublishing.com

Index